Horses

Toni Webber

Macdonald Educational

Managing Editor Chris Milsome
Editor Anne Furniss
Design Peter Benoist
Production Philip Hughes
Picture Research Lorna Collin

First published 1975
Macdonald Educational
49 Poland Street
London W1A 2LG

contents

ISBN 0 356 04458 0

Man's need for the horse

The hunter and the hunted

Millions of years ago, man hunted the horse for food. Until the end of the Stone Age, about 5,000 years ago, horsemeat was part of his main diet. Bronze Age man became the first to breed stock by capturing young horses and fattening them up for eating when food was scarce.

Once men had learned to ride, longer trips could be made in search of food. With the horse's natural speed to help him, the early hunter could pursue game until his quarry was exhausted. The horse became less important as a source of food, although mares are still milked in some parts of the world.

A means of transport

Early man soon found that horses, asses and mules made fine pack animals with their strength and willingness to work. When harnessed to litters or wheeled vehicles, they could transport whole families and all their belongings great distances in safety and comfort. Man was already beginning to find that the horse was a necessary part of his security and well-being. He continued to do so for many thousands of years.

▲ A Chinese brush drawing of a Hun archer hunting a gazelle in about 200 B.C. The Huns, a warlike tribe from the East, were very skilful horsemen. This archer has both hands on his bow and guides his horse with his knees.

◀ A Mongolian girl milking her mare. The horse has always been prized by the nomadic people in Mongolia, both to ride and as a source of food. Mare's milk may be drunk fresh or fermented to make an alcoholic drink.

▼ Transport in the Middle Ages. A French noblewoman of the 15th century drives out in a covered wagon drawn by five horses. For thousands of years, the horse provided man's fastest means of transport.

▲ An old woman in Majorca loads supplies onto her donkey. Since earliest times, all members of the horse family have been used as pack animals. The ass is a patient animal with little speed but great docility.

A **common ancestor** the dawn horse

Eohippus

Mesohippus

Merychippus

▲ The tiny "dawn horse", *Eohippus*, had flat feet with toes. The camouflage of brown stripes on its body and legs protected it in the great primaeval forests where it roamed.

▲ A few million years later, a descendant of *Eohippus* called *Mesohippus* appeared. It was a little bigger and faster, and ready to emerge from the forests to the scrubland beyond.

▲ Another step forward in the evolution of the horse. *Merychippus* gradually lost its outer toes and began to find its food on the ground in the form of grass. In size, it was as big as a calf.

A creature of the past

Sixty million years ago, a small animal no bigger than a fox moved through the undergrowth, browsing on shrubs. This small creature was the ancestor of all modern horses and is called *Eohippus*, the "dawn horse". In those days, the great continents were linked by land bridges and *Eohippus* could move freely through Europe and Asia to North America and back again.

▼ After the last Ice Age 10,000 years ago, there were four branches of the horse family left. The horse made its home mainly in Europe and northern Asia.

▼ The onager looked like a donkey but was rather bigger. It was found in the Middle East and southern Europe and was a strong animal with a vicious temper.

The missing link

When archaeologists first discovered fossilized remains of *Eohippus* in 1838 they did not realize that it was the fore-runner of the horse family. It had four toes on the front feet and three on the hind. Its teeth were shaped to eat shrubs and could never have grazed grass. In 1876, a more complete skeleton was found in America and people realized the connection.

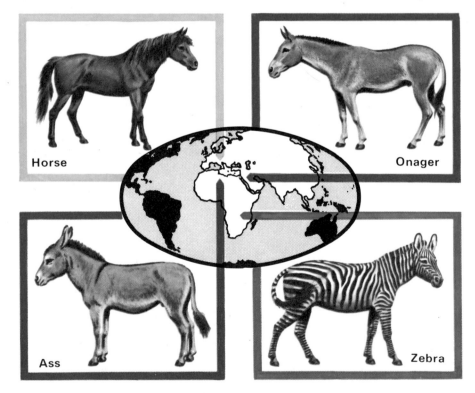

Horse

Onager

Ass

Zebra

▲ The ass lived in northern Africa and was the ancestor of our domestic donkey and the Asiatic Wild Ass. It is a strong, patient and docile animal.

▲ The zebra was the only member of the horse family which could survive the horse sickness of Africa. It has an uncertain temper but it has been tamed.

Toes become hooves

Millions of years passed and the descendants of *Eohippus* grew larger and stronger. They developed better teeth and moved out onto the plains, where grass had begun to grow.

On the open plains, these early horses were in full view of their enemies, so they needed to run faster. They found that they could achieve great speeds by running on tiptoe, and gradually their outer toes wasted away. They were left with one toe on each foot, the hoof of the modern horse.

Pliohippus

Equus caballus

▲ The first single-toed "horse", *Pliohippus*, was able to graze grass and run swiftly from enemies. Its home was the plains of North America, Asia and Europe, where it roamed freely in herds.

▲ The first true horse, *Equus caballus*, was the size of a small pony. It was a hardy little animal with a stubby mane and a stripe on its back like those of the modern Tarpan.

▼ These cave drawings at Les Combarelles in France were painted about 10,000 years ago. The paintings show that there were several different breeds of early horse.

After the end of the Ice Ages, horses developed in two basic ways. In northern regions, the temperate climate produced lush pastures. Horses became passive, heavy and slow-moving.

◄ A typical "cold blood", as they are called, is the Italian Heavy Draught Horse.

► "Hot bloods", like the Arab, are finely built and fast. They came originally from the hot, desert regions of the Middle East where grazing is poor.

Italian Heavy Draught Horse

Arab

Horses in the ancient world

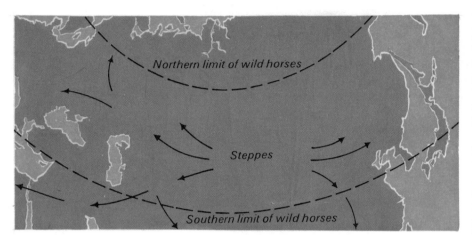

This map of ancient Asia shows where the earliest domestication of the horse took place. The nomads of the Asian steppes tamed the horse, and the art of riding spread all round the world.

▼ A Scythian warrior with his horse in ceremonial trappings. The strange reindeer mask was probably a survival from earlier tribal customs. The saddle is made from two pillows stuffed with deer hair or grass. It is worn with a saddlecloth of skins.
The bridle is leather, and both saddle and bridle are heavily decorated with felt or leather cutouts covered in gold or tin.

Wandering peoples of the steppes

Nobody really knows when the horse was first tamed, but we do know who tamed it and where. Thousands of years ago, tribes of wandering people roamed the steppes of northern Asia. Some, such as the Uryanchai, followed the herds of reindeer.

The Uryanchai relied on reindeer for milk, meat and skins for clothing. Soon, they tamed them and learned to ride. As the climate grew warmer, the reindeer moved northward, and the nomads discovered that the little steppe ponies could be tamed as easily as the reindeer. The domestication of the horse had begun.

Hordes of mounted warriors

The art of riding spread like wildfire across the open plains. Horses pulled carts loaded with possessions, carried families from place to place and bore men out to the hunt.

Groups of mounted warriors formed the first cavalry and swept down on their helpless enemies, driving all before them. A few hundred years later the first chariots appeared. These lightweight war carriages drawn by swift horses or onagers made any tribe who owned them unbeatable in the open country. Possession of the horse had become a necessity.

Frozen treasure

It is difficult now to separate truth from legend about the early horse-breeding people. But in 1947, a remarkable discovery was made in some burial mounds in northern Russia.

The graves belonged to Scythians, descendants of the people who first tamed the horse. Their tombs had flooded with water soon after closing and had frozen solid in the Arctic winter. The contents were almost perfectly preserved after 3,000 years.

In the tombs, chieftains were buried with their possessions and their horses. There were two different types of horse in the tombs. Most of the animals were small and sturdy and were obviously used to pull waggons and carry loads, but some were beautiful, tall creatures.

Saddles, bridles with primitive bits and strange decorative trappings were also found. These finds proved that the horse was highly-prized among the peoples of the ancient world.

▲ War chariots pulled by onagers are driven into battle. This frieze dates from 2500 B.C. and comes from Ur.

▼ The ancient Greeks were very skilful horsemen. They had no stirrups and often rode bareback. This scene is from a vase.

Centaur

Horse mythology

◄ There are many myths and legends about the horse. When mounted warriors first appeared from the steppes of Asia, many people thought they were strange beasts, half-man, half-horse. They named these beasts Centaurs.

► It is unlikely that there was ever a horse with wings, like Pegasus. This character from Greek mythology was thought to carry the thunder and lightning of the god Zeus.

Pegasus

The age of chivalry

Playing at war

In the early Middle Ages, rich men went to war for fun. Barons gathered together armies from their estates and travelled hundreds of miles across the sea to wars in foreign lands. When they were at home, any excuse was good enough to start a mini-war with their neighbours.

By the 13th century, however, war had lost some of its appeal. In order to protect himself, a knight had to wear such heavy armour that he could hardly move. He needed a very strong, slow-moving horse to bear his weight, and if he fell off, he had little chance of getting up again.

Kings and courtiers began to leave wars to the mercenaries, and they turned to tournaments for excitement.

Highly organized battles

Tournaments started off by being semi-organized battles between two or more barons and their men. However, this became very dangerous, so it was decided to draw up some rules.

As time went on, a code of behaviour, known as the code of chivalry, developed. Tournaments consisted of many different events, each with its own set of rules. Gradually, the tournament changed from a rowdy battle into a highly organized sport for competitors and spectators.

Horses in the Middle Ages

There were a number of different horses in general use in the Middle Ages. The horse was a sign of a man's prosperity or status, rather like the car today.

Ladies and priests rode *ambling palfreys,* which were small elegant horses that were very comfortable to ride.

The knight would ride a *destrier* in battle and at a tournament, while his squire was mounted on a *rouncy*. This was a cob-like animal which was also used by merchants and bailiffs.

Yeomen rode *hobies,* which were small, solid yet agile ponies.

Servants were mounted on *nags:* rather coarsely-bred horses.

▼ Tournaments were early spectator sports, organized as carefully as football matches are today. They usually took place in a stadium set up outside a town. Stands and tents were set up for spectators and an area cleared for competitors. The space in which the events took place was called the lists.

▼ The horse that the knight rode was called a destrier, from the Latin *dexter,* meaning right. This was because the horses were trained to turn away to the right at the end of the lists. They were powerful, heavy animals, which had to be capable of carrying a knight in full armour down the lists at a gallop.

▼ The only people allowed in the lists were the competitors, their squires and the judges. The knights charged at each other down either side of a high fence. The object was to unhorse your opponent with your lance. Once one knight had fallen off, the fight sometimes continued on the ground.

◀ Knights competed either for money, for honour or for the favours of a lady. They had to swear before competing to follow the code of chivalry, but sometimes they would try to cheat in order to win. An accusation of cheating was a terrible insult, so there was always a presiding judge whose decision must be accepted.

◀ Very few men could afford to enter a tournament. They were usually noblemen who were rich enough to bear the cost of several horses, a squire and much costly equipment. Each knight had a coat of arms or other heraldic symbol which he wore on his head piece, on his armour and on the trappings of his horse and his servants.

9

Battle cry! The horse at war

▲ The Egyptian pharaoh, Rameses II, goes to war in his chariot. He has both hands free for his bow and arrow. On the left, a farmer tries to remove his cattle from the scene of battle.

▶ Warfare in 841 A.D. The invention of the stirrup in the sixth century in Mongolia had a great effect on mounted warfare. Men could now stand up in the saddle to fight.

▼ Eastern warriors were often fantastic horsemen. They practically lived in the saddle, and trained their horses to gallop flat out at the enemy, turning away at the last moment.

Chariots and chargers

For nearly 5,000 years, the horse was driven or ridden to war. The early civilizations of the world were brought down by hordes of barbarians on horseback or in horse-drawn chariots.

In Europe, heavy horses bore armoured knights into battle in thunderous charges which trampled all before them. But the heavy cavalry were at a loss when they met Eastern warriors on their speedy, hot-blooded ponies. These skilful horsemen would never meet heavy cavalry in a charge, but galloped circles around them, constantly firing arrows.

Bad horsemanship

17th and 18th century paintings of dashing horsemen charging into battle are often flattering but untruthful. Most cavalry troopers were just about able to stay on their horses in a charge, but quite unable to reform afterwards. Only a few regiments, such as the Cossacks, really knew how to use the speed and agility of the horse in battle.

▲ The last appearance of the horse on the field of battle was in World War II. They stood no chance against modern weapons such as the tank.

The strength of the cavalry in battle was its ability to attack at speed and surprise. The illustrations on this page show the Battle of Blenheim, in which the cavalry played an important part. The battle took place in 1704 between the French and Bavarians under Marshal Tallard and an Allied army under the Duke of Marlborough.

Battle of Blenheim

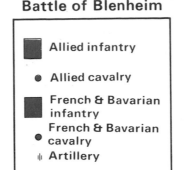

■ Allied infantry

● Allied cavalry

■ French & Bavarian infantry

● French & Bavarian cavalry

⫿ Artillery

English trooper

French carabinier

12 noon

Oberglau

Lutzingen

Blenheim

main road

N

0   1
km.

▲ At the start of the battle, the two armies are drawn up on either side of the river Nebel. Marlborough, the commander of the Allied army, attacks at either end of the French and Bavarian army in order to drain their resources from the centre.

◄ Most of the French and Bavarian infantry are drawn into the villages of Blenheim and Oberglau to defend them from fierce Allied attacks. Meanwhile, Allied infantry press forward across the river Nebel and hold the crossings for the cavalry.

► Gunfire and successive cavalry charges destroy the French infantry holding the centre. Allied cavalry storm through the gap, driving the French cavalry before them. The French and Bavarian army is divided and surrounded by the victorious Allies.

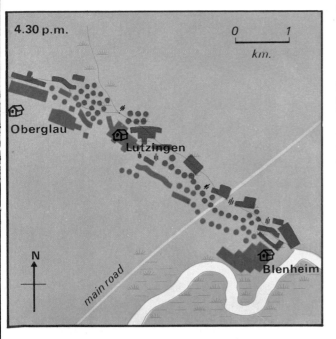

4.30 p.m.

Oberglau

Lutzingen

Blenheim

main road

N

0   1
km.

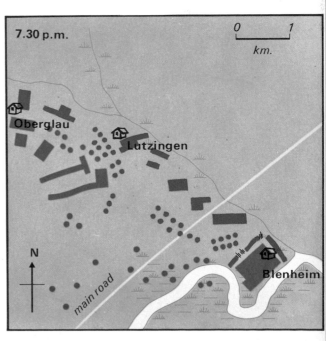

7.30 p.m.

Oberglau

Lutzingen

Blenheim

main road

N

0   1
km.

Messengers on horseback

▲ A private courier carries important messages abroad in the 17th century.

Riding hell for leather

A ruler can only govern a large empire successfully if he can keep in touch with his outlying armies. He needs instant news of uprisings or of triumphs or defeats in war. For this, a fast and regular messenger system is vitally important. The first people to set up such a system were the Persians in about 400 B.C.

At that time the Persian empire was ruled by King Cyrus and stretched from Egypt to the Indus river. Cyrus organized a series of relay stations, allowing one day's ride to each man and horse. He used the fleet-footed Bactrian horses, the ancestors of the modern Arab. For the next 2,000 years, all important messages were carried on horseback.

The fastest method of travel

There was no public system for sending messages before the 17th century. Until then, messages could only be sent by private messenger, and this was very expensive.

Most countries set up postal systems in the 17th century. At first, these were relays of men on horseback, but they were soon replaced by fast coaches drawn by teams of horses.

Posting stations were set up where the horses could be changed by expert ostlers in a few minutes, and mail coaches began to take private passengers. Until the railways were built, the mail coach was the fastest method of public transport.

The Pony Express

For 18 months in the mid-19th century, the Pony Express carried the mail across 3,219 km. (2,000 miles) of wild country in the United States. The exploits of their brave riders made them famous throughout the world.

San Francisco

Sacramento

Salt Lake City

▲ Pony Express riders had to face hostile Indians, swollen rivers and terrible weather, but they covered the distance in 10 days.

◄ William F. Cody, the famous Buffalo Bill, was only 15 when he joined the Pony Express. He set the record for the longest ride: 618 km. (384 miles).

Speed records

▶ This illustration compares the speed records of a man with those of a single rider and a coach drawn by a team of horses.

A man running can only average 8.5 k.p.h. (5 m.p.h.) over a long distance. A coach drawn by a team can more than double this speed, but only with several changes of horses.

The fastest speeds have been set by single riders on relays of horses. In 1820, a man covered 322 km. (200 miles) in 8½ hrs, an average speed of 37 k.p.h. (23 m.p.h.).

In desperate cases, men have had to travel hundreds of miles flat out on only one horse. This is known as "riding to death"

Man running
8.5 k.p.h.

Coach and horses
20 k.p.h.

Horseman
37 k.p.h.

▶ The first Pony Express rider leaves St Joseph, Missouri, on April 3, 1860. His name was Johnson Richardson and his pony a bright bay mare. Souvenir hunters in the gaily decorated town plucked hairs from her tail, and a cannon salute sped the rider on his way.

▲ The spanning of the West. Somewhere east of Salt Lake City, two riders pass in mid-journey. There was no time to stop. The motto of the Pony Express, "the mail must go through", made each rider determined to carry on without delay.

● St. Joseph

▶ The mail was carried in four pouches stitched to the corners of a heavy leather saddle cloth, called a *mochila*. The *mochila* had a hole for the saddle horn and a slit for the cantle, and could be quickly transferred from one horse to another.

◀ When the "talking wires" were finally joined in July, 1861, it was the beginning of the end for the Pony Express. The telegraph could carry messages across the continent in a matter of minutes. But the crews erecting telegraph poles were a welcome sight to the lonely riders as they raced along the trail.

Pony Express saddle

The Mochila

Roads through the ages

▲ This cross section of a Roman road shows how well the Romans understood road-building. They built roads in layers, using heavy material on the bottom layer and making use of local materials. Rainwater ran into drains on either side.

▲ For 1,000 years, the Roman skills were forgotten. Roads collapsed from neglect. Ruts appeared in wet weather, dried out and cracked in the summer and got worse again in winter. Travel was slow and dangerous. Passengers often had to get out and walk.

▲ Towards the end of the 18th century, road construction got better. The new roads were made with the natural earth, which was pounded to make a hard base. Packed rubble or gravel was laid on top to provide a smooth surface and good drainage.

▲ The elaborately decorated dress chariot of the early 19th century was the equivalent of today's Rolls-Royce. It was used by the rich and on special occasions. The vehicle was painted in the family colours and driven by a coachman in livery. The horses were well-matched and quite sturdy, often of German stock.

▼ Nowadays, the family car is the most common vehicle on the road, but in the past very few people could afford the expense of a coach and horses. If they could, it would be a plain and serviceable carriage, capable of carrying a man and his wife with several children and all their luggage.

Early wheeled vehicles

Ever since man first tamed the horse, he has used these strong and willing animals to pull wheeled vehicles. For hundreds of years, these vehicles were either fast, two-wheeled war chariots or solid, slow country carts with four wheels.

In the 16th century, some Hungarian wainwrights introduced a new design in wagon building. They put small wheels on the front axle and larger ones behind. This meant that they could be driven from a box at the front instead of by a postilion on one of the horses. The new vehicle was faster and much easier to handle than the clumsy cart. It was quickly copied by designers and builders all over Europe.

Laws against the coach

People everywhere were enthusiastic about the new "coach", as it was called. But the excitement alarmed many governments. They thought the art of horsemanship would die out and that carriage horses might replace riding horses.

They feared that in times of war there would be no suitable horses or horsemen to call upon. Some states passed laws against the coach, and statesmen even described coach travel as unmanly.

However, coach travel had come to stay. At the end of the 18th century, new techniques for building roads were introduced, and the age of horsedrawn transport reached the height of its popularity.

▼ The stage coach carried passengers on short and long journeys on regular routes with organized stops, or stages. The horses were chosen for stamina because they had to pull a heavy load quite fast for hours on end. Unlike the modern motor coach, an armed guard sat up behind.

▲ The farmer needs transport for many reasons. The modern pick-up truck or Land Rover takes him around his land, carries passengers, dogs and goods to market. In the past, a large, open cart drawn by one heavy horse would be used.

▶ The curricle of the early 19th century held the same position among horse-drawn vehicles as the Ferrari holds among cars. They were very expensive and fast and drawn by beautifully-matched, fast horses with Arab blood. Curricles were usually owned by rich young men who drove them with dash and speed along public roads, much to the annoyance of more sober people.

The blacksmith care of the horse

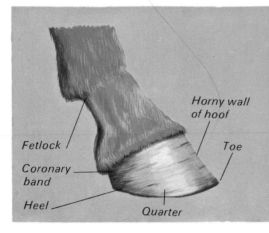

The horse's hoof

◀ Side view of a horse's foot. The feet have to bear constant weight, so they must be strong, flexible and able to absorb shock. The horny wall of the hoof grows downward from the coronary band and protects the foot.

Fetlock

Coronary band

Heel

Horny wall of hoof

Toe

Quarter

▶ The underside of the hoof. The V-shaped frog is most important as it absorbs shock and prevents the horse slipping. It is made of rubbery horn and supported by the bars. The sole is concave to help the horse grip.

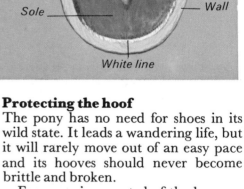

Frog

Bars

Sole

Wall

White line

Horseshoes

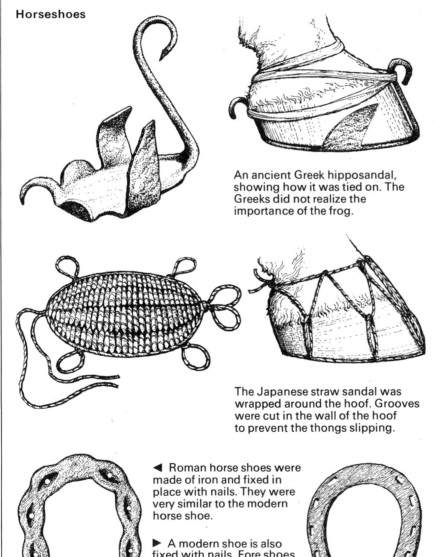

An ancient Greek hipposandal, showing how it was tied on. The Greeks did not realize the importance of the frog.

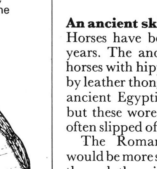

The Japanese straw sandal was wrapped around the hoof. Grooves were cut in the wall of the hoof to prevent the thongs slipping.

◀ Roman horse shoes were made of iron and fixed in place with nails. They were very similar to the modern horse shoe.

▶ A modern shoe is also fixed with nails. Fore shoes also have a clip at the front, while hind shoes have clips on either side.

Protecting the hoof

The pony has no need for shoes in its wild state. It leads a wandering life, but it will rarely move out of an easy pace and its hooves should never become brittle and broken.

Far more is expected of the horse or pony which is domesticated. Some of its work will be on hard roads and its daily routine may be very tough. The strain on its feet will be enormous. To help protect its feet, a horse needs shoes.

An ancient skill

Horses have been shod for over 2,000 years. The ancient Greeks fitted their horses with hippo-sandals, kept in place by leather thongs. The Japanese and the ancient Egyptians used straw sandals, but these wore down very quickly and often slipped off.

The Romans realized that shoes would be more secure if nails were driven through them into the horny part of the hoof. This method is still in use.

The role of the blacksmith

Until recently, there was a forge in every village, and certainly one within easy reach of every horse. Today, however, village smithies are few and far between, and instead of the horse going to the blacksmith, the blacksmith must come to the horse.

The blacksmith's job is therefore more complicated. He can make the shoe in his forge, travel to the horse and fit it on cold, but it might not fit perfectly. To overcome this problem, many smiths now have small forges which they carry with them. In this way, they can fit and make each shoe on the spot.

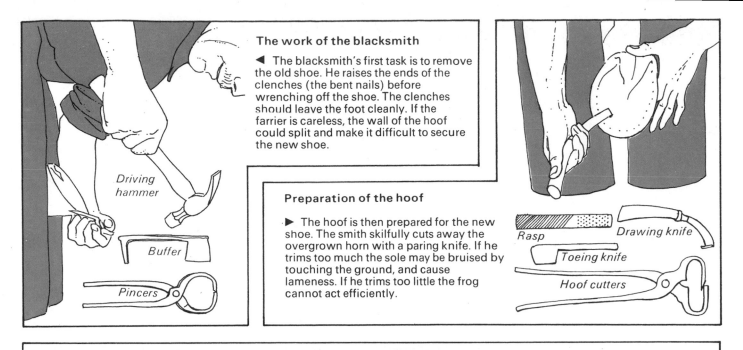

The work of the blacksmith

◄ The blacksmith's first task is to remove the old shoe. He raises the ends of the clenches (the bent nails) before wrenching off the shoe. The clenches should leave the foot cleanly. If the farrier is careless, the wall of the hoof could split and make it difficult to secure the new shoe.

Driving hammer

Buffer

Pincers

Preparation of the hoof

▶ The hoof is then prepared for the new shoe. The smith skilfully cuts away the overgrown horn with a paring knife. If he trims too much the sole may be bruised by touching the ground, and cause lameness. If he trims too little the frog cannot act efficiently.

Rasp   *Drawing knife*

Toeing knife

Hoof cutters

Making the shoe

◄ The smith turns the red-hot shoe on the anvil to achieve a perfect fit. From time to time, he holds the hot shoe against the hoof to check how much adjustment is needed. The metal is heated in the fire to make it soft and workable. It is cooled by dunking in cold water. The metal used is fullered iron (iron with a groove along one side).

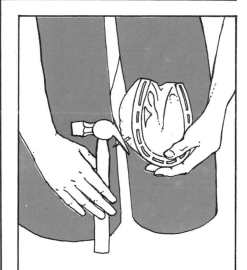

The shoe is fitted

▲ The final stage is to nail the shoe in place. The nails, or clenches, are driven right through the wall of the hoof. The ends are twisted off, bent over and hammered down. The smith must be careful not to place the nails too close to the sole. If it is damaged it may cause lameness. Finally, the hoof is rasped and painted with oil.

The horse and its rider

Riding styles

◀ The short riding style. The rider's knee is bent and the ball of his foot rests on the stirrup. The object is to bring the rider's centre of gravity forward in line with that of the horse.

▶ The long, straight-legged style of the cowboy. The seat of the saddle slopes backwards to support the rider. Riding this way is less tiring over long distances.

How the horse moves

▲ A Lusitano horse, from Portugal, trots around a paddock. It has a high-stepping action, much favoured in harness horses. The horse's natural paces are the walk, the trot, the canter and the fast canter or gallop.

▶ For the natural paces, the horse moves its legs in a diagonal pattern, as shown in the diagram. The near side fore foot is followed by the off side hind, then the off side fore and the near side hind.

▶ The amble is an artificial gait, in which both feet on one side touch the ground before the feet on the other. Some horses are trained to the gait, while others have an inborn tendency to amble. An ambling horse is very comfortable to ride, particularly over long distances.

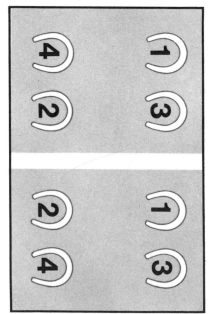

Controlling the horse

Every item worn by the well turned-out pony or horse of today has a practical purpose. The first man to ride a horse rode bareback and clung to the animal's mane. But people soon found better ways to control this new method of transport.

Early bridles were just pieces of rope tied around the horse's lower jaw. Now, the horse is controlled by means of a bit which is held in its mouth by the bridle. Pressure on the rein causes the bit to act on the horse's mouth. With some bits, pressure acts on the whole head.

Support for the rider

Saddles have been used since earliest times, for the comfort of both horse and rider. The underside is padded so that the weight of the rider is carried on the muscular part of the back and not on the backbone.

A saddle is designed to suit the needs of the rider. The cowboy saddle may seem elaborate, but every part has a use. It supports the rider and enables him to carry equipment. Old war saddles were solid and built up at back and front to support a man in armour.

The invention of the stirrup was very important as the rider no longer had to struggle to keep his balance. Stirrup shapes have varied enormously over the years and have often changed with the fashion in shoes.

Even riding styles have changed. Nowadays, most people ride "short", with their knees bent and their hands held low. But the rancher who spends long hours in the saddle will still ride "long", sitting well back in the saddle with a straight leg.

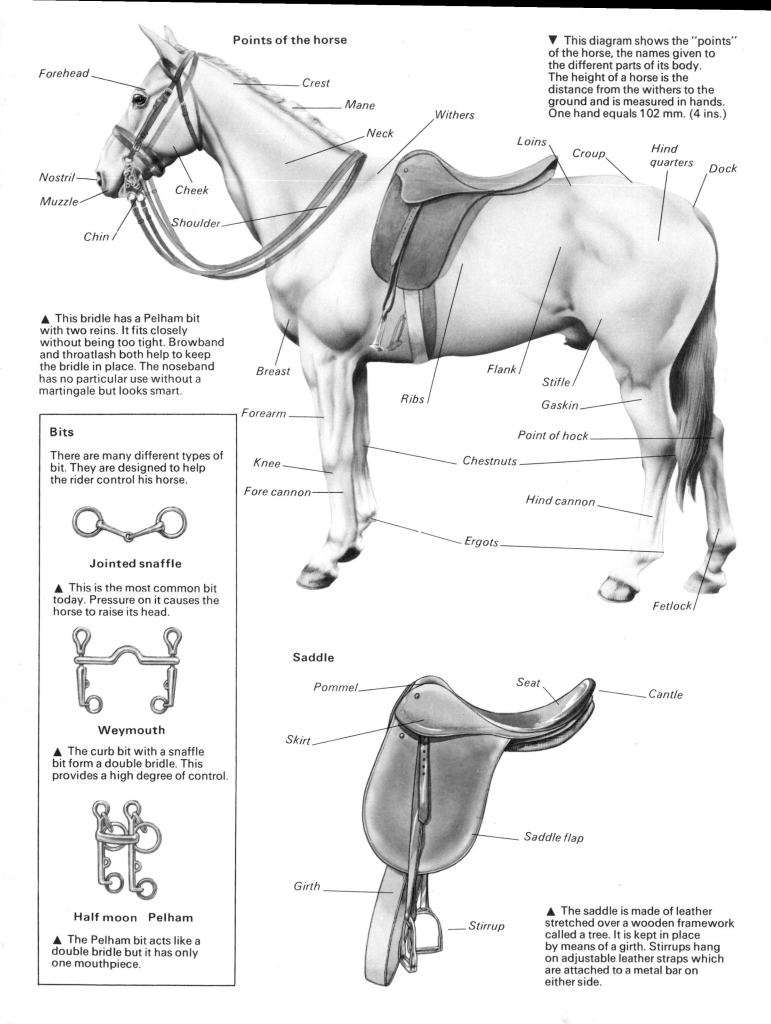

Points of the horse

Forehead

Crest

Mane

Neck

Withers

Nostril

Muzzle

Cheek

Chin

Shoulder

Loins

Croup

Hind quarters

Dock

▼ This diagram shows the "points" of the horse, the names given to the different parts of its body. The height of a horse is the distance from the withers to the ground and is measured in hands. One hand equals 102 mm. (4 ins.)

▲ This bridle has a Pelham bit with two reins. It fits closely without being too tight. Browband and throatlash both help to keep the bridle in place. The noseband has no particular use without a martingale but looks smart.

Breast

Forearm

Knee

Fore cannon

Ribs

Flank

Stifle

Gaskin

Point of hock

Chestnuts

Hind cannon

Ergots

Fetlock

Bits

There are many different types of bit. They are designed to help the rider control his horse.

Jointed snaffle

▲ This is the most common bit today. Pressure on it causes the horse to raise its head.

Weymouth

▲ The curb bit with a snaffle bit form a double bridle. This provides a high degree of control.

Half moon   Pelham

▲ The Pelham bit acts like a double bridle but it has only one mouthpiece.

Saddle

Pommel

Seat

Cantle

Skirt

Saddle flap

Girth

Stirrup

▲ The saddle is made of leather stretched over a wooden framework called a tree. It is kept in place by means of a girth. Stirrups hang on adjustable leather straps which are attached to a metal bar on either side.

Running wild

Prjevalski's horse
▶ Prjevalski's horse is a direct link with the Ice Age. It is the only truly wild pony in the world today. It is small, with an erect mane and faint stripes on its back and legs.

The world's "wild" horses
The only true wild horse in the world today is Prjevalski's Horse, named after the man who discovered it at the end of the last century in Mongolia. They are genuinely wild because their ancestors have never been tamed.

All other herds of "wild" horses and ponies live in carefully controlled freedom. The Tarpan survived without help until the end of the last century, but was taken into captivity as it was in danger of extinction.

Many countries have herds of semi-wild ponies. In France, beautiful white horses roam the Camargue. Dulmen horses live on a reserve in Germany and Gotland ponies live "wild" on Logsta Hed moor in Sweden. In Britain, there are as many as eight breeds of semi-wild pony.

Life in the wild
Nowadays, these semi-wild ponies have no natural enemies. They band together in herds and move at will over their territory, grazing from time to time. At night, they sleep standing up, keeping close together for comfort and from an old instinct for safety.

Semi-wild ponies are tough little animals with shaggy coats who can withstand very bad weather. The wind is more trouble to them than rain, snow or frost; they seek shelter huddled together in a natural hollow or behind a windbreak.

Although they fend for themselves, the ponies are carefully watched by their human keepers. Food is provided during times of thick snow and they are regularly rounded up, counted and branded.

▲ New Forest ponies wander through a clearing in the forest in England. The foal is only a few hours old, but it was born with its eyes open and can immediately stand up and follow its mother.

▶ Round-ups, or drifts, are held each autumn in the New Forest. The ponies are herded into fenced enclosures where they are counted, sorted and branded. Some of the foals are removed and sold.

◄ Two ponies feeding in a shallow pond amid the beautiful New Forest scenery. The ponies roam freely all over the forest land and are unmoved by people or cars.

► At the age of six months, all foals are branded with a number and the mark of their owner.

▼ A New Forest keeper burns off old gorse and heather. This is done every March to provide the ponies with fresh herbage. Newly burnt gorse stems are a favourite meal of the ponies.

► New Forest ponies feed on hay which was left for them after a heavy fall of snow. In bad winters, hay is brought in by tractor or dropped by helicopter on the open forest. The ponies are capable of scratching through the snow to the grass beneath, but this does not provide very good feeding.

Wide open spaces farmer and stockman

◀ Mongolian herdsmen usually ride hardy, sure-footed hill ponies. They can withstand many degrees of frost and survive on poor food. The Mongol saddle has changed little since it was first used over 2,000 years ago. It has a high pommel (front) and cantle (rear) and is elaborately decorated.

▼ The Mounties are now seen in traditional uniform only at ceremonies. They still "get their man", but with helicopters, not with horses.

▶ An Australian farmer tends his sheep and his horse waits patiently. On larger ranches, a horse is still the best method of transport for the farmer.

Herding and protecting stock

Wherever there are great areas of land to cover and large herds of animals to protect, the horse is important to man. On the vast ranches of America, Australia and New Zealand it is unlikely that the horse will ever give way to mechanized transport.

Riding in these areas calls for great skill. In some parts of Australia, for example, the terrain is so rough that any speed faster than a walk would seem dangerous. Yet the Aboriginal stockman will drive cattle at a gallop, often riding bareback.

Keeping law and order

In some open places, the police still patrol on horseback. In Africa, the Lesotho Mounted Police track cattle rustlers, and in the Australian outback policemen on horseback are more useful than car patrols. But the most famous mounted policeman of all, the Royal Canadian Mounted Police, now use their horses only for ceremonial events.

◄ A Mexican cowhand rides out on horseback to bring in his cattle. All the equipment he may need is carried on his saddle.

► The South American gauchos are fine horsemen who learn to ride almost before they can walk. They wear loose-fitting clothes for comfort when riding and their most prized possessions are a silver knife and a *rastra,* a broad belt covered with silver coins.

The saddle has no horn, so the gaucho jams the end of his lasso under the stirrup leather when roping a steer. Wide, decorated stirrups protect the feet from the thorny undergrowth.

The city horse

19th century city stables

◄ Where land was scarce in the centre of a city, horses were kept in two storey stables, with a ramp leading to the upper floors. Working horses were well fed and usually bedded down on best straw, soft peat or wood shavings.

Funeral coach

▼ The fire engine was always drawn by grey horses because they were conspicuous. In contrast, horses for funerals were known as the "black brigade". They were chosen for their generous natures and placid temperament.

Fire engine

All sorts of horses

If you could suddenly go back in time 100 years and stand in a street in any town or city, one of the first things you would notice would be the horses.

Horses of every shape, size and colour would be everywhere, singly or in teams, smart or scruffy, young or old. A large city in the last century might contain as many as 300,000 horses, as well as several thousand donkeys and mules.

Nowadays, if you want to see horse-drawn vehicles going about their daily work, a city may still be the best place to find them. Many businesses are beginning to use horses again, either for advertisement or for convenience. At least a horse can be relied upon to start on a cold, wet winter morning.

◀ Horse-drawn cabs are available in many cities for the use of tourists. This one is in Rome. The cab horses may be of any breed; in North African resorts, they are often Arabs, but European horses are used elsewhere.

▼ Road surfaces in the city varied from street to street, and the change from one surface to another meant that the horse was continually changing its pace. The worst surface was asphalt, particularly when it was wet, for it was difficult for a heavily laden horse to keep its footing. The best surface was wood sprinkled with gravel.

▼ The horses which pulled buses and delivery carts had a hard life. They were usually country bred horses which were chosen for their sturdy build.

Delivery cart

Horse-drawn omnibus

Hackney cab

Horse power

We still use the term "horse power" to describe the power of an engine, even though horses as a source of energy have almost completely disappeared from the industrial scene. The term "horse power" originally referred to the number of horses which were needed to pull a steam engine when it was taken from place to place.

Before the development of the steam engine, the strength of the horse was needed to operate all sorts of machinery. No workyard or farm was complete without horse gear, a contraption to which the horse was harnessed.

Horse gear could be fitted to many different types of machine, such as butter churns, threshing machines and the grinding stones of a mill. The shaft could be linked to pulleys and used in earth moving. Horses were even used at the seaside for hauling bathing machines in and out of the sea.

▲ A tiny donkey plods along under an enormous load of sponges. In fact, the load probably does not weigh very much, but it must have been difficult to balance it on the donkey's back.

▶ The life of a barge horse was not usually very hard unless the barge itself was heavily loaded. The bargee or a member of his family would lead the horse along the towpath of the canal. When they came to a lock, the horse would be unhitched while the barge was winched through.

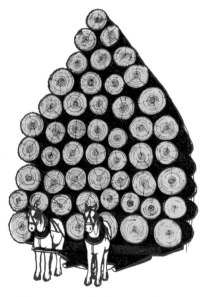

▲ The heaviest load ever pulled by two horses. It was in 1893 in Michigan, U.S.A. The 50 logs on the sledge weigh 54.6 tonnes (53.8 tons).

▶ Pit ponies are led to work in a coal mine, wearing bridles with protective eye guards. There are very few ponies working in the pits now. They live in underground stables but often come to the surface for holidays.

Hauling heavy loads

It was not only to work machinery that the horse was needed in the past. Wherever there were heavy loads to be moved, the horse could be found.

Long before the railways appeared, wagons that ran on rails were developed for use in mines and early factories. They were nearly always pulled by horses or, in the mines, by tough little ponies such as the Shetland and the Galloway.

Today, many of the traditional jobs of the horse have been taken over by mechanized equipment. But the horse is still highly valued in primitive or mountainous regions where tracks are impassable to wheeled vehicles or the people are too poor to own them.

In these areas, the docile donkey comes into its own as a beast of burden. Another useful animal is the mule, which is the offspring of a mare and a donkey stallion.

Horse-powered butter churn

▲ This horse is attached by the collar to an overhead wheel which works a butter churn. Most horse power worked on the same principle, with the horse plodding endlessly round in circles.

Portable farm engine

▲ The development of the steam engine marked the decline of the horse in industry. But for some years teams of horses pulled the engines from place to place. They sometimes pulled engines along the roads so that the strange machines did not frighten other horse-drawn transport.

◄ 20th century horse power in Greece. A modern Greek farmer still threshes corn by a method used by his ancestors for generations. The horse is attached to the central post by a leading rein. When it reaches the end of the rein, it goes the other way.

Gentle giants heavy horses

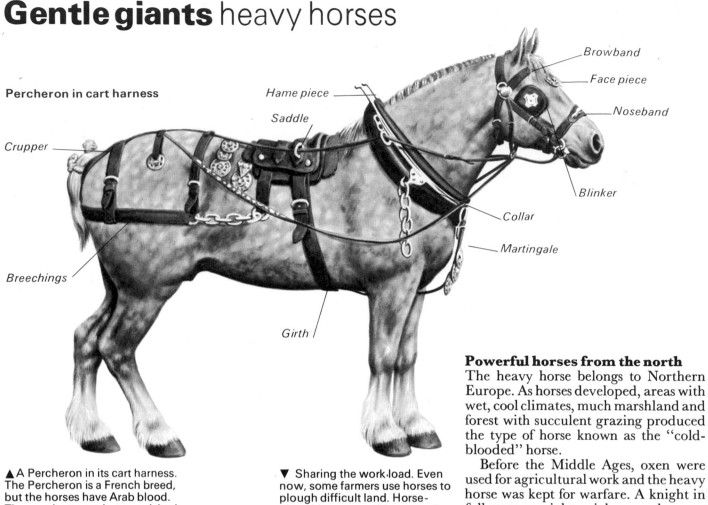

Percheron in cart harness

Crupper

Breechings

Girth

Hame piece

Saddle

Browband

Face piece

Noseband

Blinker

Collar

Martingale

▲ A Percheron in its cart harness. The Percheron is a French breed, but the horses have Arab blood. They are immense but surprisingly agile.

▼ Sharing the work load. Even now, some farmers use horses to plough difficult land. Horse-ploughing competitions are also becoming very popular.

Powerful horses from the north

The heavy horse belongs to Northern Europe. As horses developed, areas with wet, cool climates, much marshland and forest with succulent grazing produced the type of horse known as the "cold-blooded" horse.

Before the Middle Ages, oxen were used for agricultural work and the heavy horse was kept for warfare. A knight in full armour might weigh as much as 200 kg. (31 stone), and his horse would wear armour as well. The only horses which could bear this weight and still charge into battle were the hefty cold-blooded breeds.

At work on the farm

The cold-bloods became the best labourers. They are immensely strong, hugely built and extraordinarily docile. Today, France has the largest number of heavy breeds and most of them still work on farms in the way they have done for centuries.

Unfortunately, in most of Northern Europe the use of the heavy horse on the farm has declined. But the horses themselves show no signs of dying out. Their breeding is now carefully controlled to preserve the purity and qualities of each breed. The largest heavy horse of all is the Shire, which sometimes reaches a height of 18 hands.

Nowadays, heavy horses can be seen at work in the country and sometimes in cities. They still have their advantages. A horse is cheaper to run than a truck and it will not skid on icy roads. If necessary, it can even find its way home without help from the driver.

▲ Resting at the end of the day. Heavy horse societies have done much to preserve the purity of the many breeds. Some farmers have even given up their tractors, finding that horses are cheaper and more reliable for farm work.

◄ A horse helps a lumberman by pulling logs through the woods. Heavy timber is often best hauled by horses, especially in places where it would be difficult or impossible to take wheeled vehicles.

▼ A brewer's dray with matched horses at a country fair. The large breweries are keen breeders of the heavy horse. The beautifully turned-out teams are a good advertisement as well as being useful.

Horse brasses

Horse brasses are worn on harnesses and date from very early times. They were originally magic charms to ward off evil spirits.

▲ The sun is one of the earliest symbols of good fortune. This brass shows a sun with radiant arms set in a pierced wheel.

▲ A brass bell set in the shape of a crescent. Throughout the world, noise is used to frighten away evil spirits.

▲ Horse brasses often reflected the work of the horse. This brass would have been worn by a horse which pulled railway trucks.

Heavenly horses from the East

◀ A flying horse standing on a swallow. This Chinese bronze of a horse was made in about 200 A.D. With its high head and tail carriage, this horse is typical of the famous "heavenly horses" of Ferghana.

Blood-sweating horses

Two thousand years ago, Chinese merchants who followed the ancient trade routes across Asia returned home with some strange tales. They told of wonderful horses they had seen in Ferghana in central Asia. These horses were tall, golden in colour and as swift as the wind, and were said to sweat blood.

Compared with the small, slow ponies of most of the ancient world, these exotic, hot-blooded creatures must have seemed like gifts from the gods. Possession of them would surely mean victory in any battle.

More valuable than gold

The people of Ferghana would not part with their horses, even when the Emperor Wu offered them a gift of a solid gold horse. Eventually, he sent an army against them which captured some of the horses and carried them back to China.

Gradually, the horses spread across Asia and into the west, either through trade or with conquering armies. They were crossed with local mares in every country and are the ancestors of all today's light or "hot-blooded" breeds.

▼ This map shows how the hot-blooded horse spread from its homeland in Ferghana all over Asia and Europe.

▶ This 16th century Persian miniature shows courtiers mounted on hot-blooded horses with "dish" profiles like the modern Arab.

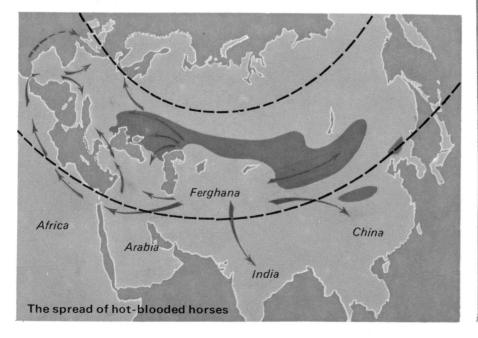

Africa

Arabia

Ferghana

India

China

The spread of hot-blooded horses

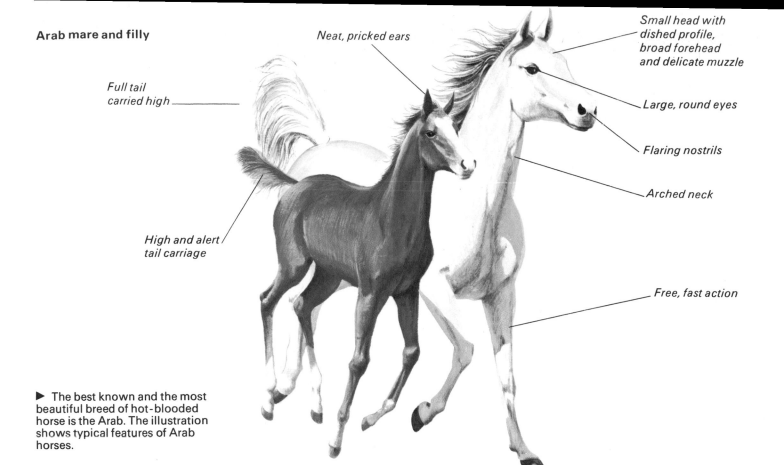

Arab mare and filly

Neat, pricked ears

Small head with dished profile, broad forehead and delicate muzzle

Full tail carried high

Large, round eyes

Flaring nostrils

Arched neck

High and alert tail carriage

Free, fast action

▶ The best known and the most beautiful breed of hot-blooded horse is the Arab. The illustration shows typical features of Arab horses.

Hot-blooded horses today

▲ A peasant with his Kurdish stallion in Persia. These horses are descended from the ancient horses of Ferghana and crossed with local breeds. The large eyes and high tail carriage show that it is a close relative of the Arab.

◀ Bedouin tribesmen taking part in a ceremonial gathering in Morocco. For more than 1,000 years, his horse has been one of the Arab's most important possessions. The horse is treated as a member of the family. It is hand-fed on scraps and allowed in the tent at night. In return, it gives its master unswerving loyalty.

The horse returns to America

Conquering new lands

By the end of the last Ice Age, the horse had disappeared in North America and for 10,000 years the continent had no horses. The first to arrive were brought to Mexico by Cortez and his Spanish *conquistadores*. There were 15 horses and two foals in the expedition and these strange beasts amazed and terrified the native Indians.

Living wild and free

As the Spaniards moved north into the land which is now the United States, some of their horses escaped. Gradually these wild horses, or mustangs as they were called, formed great herds and roamed the plains.

Living wild made the horses coarser but gave them great powers of endurance. They were captured and tamed by the Indians and later by the European settlers who crossed the plains to open up the West.

Horses also came to America with the early settlers on the east coast and were crossed with wild mustangs and with imported Thoroughbreds. Their descendants, today's American breeds, combine the pride and strength of the wild mustang and the intelligence and good looks of the Thoroughbred.

The horses of Cortez

◄ A Mexican Indian is speared by a Spaniard on horseback. The Indians had never seen horses before and were terrified. They thought the animals were monsters, half-man half-beast, like the centaurs of ancient Greece. In fact, the Spanish horses were Andalusians, a cross between Arab horses and native Spanish breeds.

Blackfoot *travois*

▲ A woman of the Blackfoot tribe with a *travois,* a kind of litter. It was made of wood poles lashed together in the form of an "A" and used to transport possessions, old people and children. The ends of the poles dragged on the ground and soon wore down.

The Indians of the American plains were quick to take advantage of the horse. They saw how useful it would be for hunting and transport as well as for war. They captured colts and yearlings from wild herds and from the Spaniards, and quickly became skilled horsemen.

◄ An example of Comanche horsemanship. Some Indian tribes developed tremendous skill on horseback. They rode into battle bareback with only a piece of rope tied around the horse's lower jaw as a bridle.

American breeds

▲ The American Saddle horse is a breed which developed in the southern states of the U.S. Rich plantation owners wanted horses which were beautiful and intelligent but strong and comfortable enough to ride for hours.

▶ The Quarter horse is famous throughout the world for its popularity with the cowboys of the wild west. No breed can equal its skill when rounding up cattle. But its name comes from earlier times, when it was used for quarter-mile races in the streets of colonial towns.

Nez Percé Appaloosa

▲ A Nez Percé Indian on a spotted, or Appaloosa, horse. All Indians were fascinated by coloured horses, particularly skewbalds and pintos. The Nez Percé were the first to breed them specially, and their Appaloosas were greatly prized.

An Indian buffalo hide decorated with drawings of horses.
The horse was most useful to the Indians for hunting buffalo. The buffalo was vital to them as a source of food, clothing and even furniture. Before the Indians had horses, the hunt was a long and difficult task. With the horse, they could chase buffalo and spear or shoot them.

33

Rodeo !

Big business

Today, rodeos are very popular and are held all over the United States and in Canada. Some of the contests go back to the cowboy's original work on the range. Others, like bareback riding, bull riding and steer wrestling, were introduced more recently as the rodeo developed. All the trials require strength and great skill, but the rewards for a successful rodeo rider are high.

The judges mark the performance of the bucking bronco or the bull as well as that of the rider. This means that it is important to find mounts that are cunning and will buck really hard. A good horse is hard to come by and may cost as much as $4,500 (about £2,000).

Trials of skill

A cowboy's life in the old Wild West was hard. Long hours were spent in the saddle, watching over the cattle. On branding days, calves had to be separated from the herd and their owners' mark put on with a hot iron. At nightfall, if a cowboy was far from home, he slept on the ground using a saddle as a pillow.

The main event of the season was the move to the nearest railhead. Usually, several herds arrived together and this was a good opportunity for the cowboys to relax and have some fun. They often arranged contests, using the skills from which they made a living. These friendly competitions were the first rodeos.

▲ A moment of relaxation in a hard working life. 19th century cowboys take the opportunity to wash off the dust of the trail with a dip in a waterhole.

Bareback riding

Chaps

Spurs

Rigging

▲ A bareback rider clings to the handhold on the leather pad which is all that a bareback bronco wears. The rider must stay on his mount for 8 or 10 seconds. His free hand must not touch horse or equipment. The higher and wilder he spurs, the better his marking. The contest dates from the days when cowboys broke wild mustangs in for work on the ranch.

▲ Calf roping is one of the oldest contests in the rodeo. The man lassoes the calf, leaps from his horse and throws the calf to the ground by hand. Quarter horses are used for this event because they have good "cow sense".

▲ A 19th century poster advertising Buffalo Bill's rodeo show. William F. Cody was a great showman and the first to turn the work of the cowboy into show business. His performers included Indians, stage coaches and buffalo.

▶ Steer wrestling. In this contest the rider leaps from his horse, grabs the steer by horn and jaw and throws it to the ground. The other horse and rider are there to make sure the steer runs in a straight line.

▼ Chuck wagon racing at Canada's most famous rodeo, the Calgary Stampede. As in the chariot races of ancient Rome, the drivers must be both brave and very skilful in handling their teams of four horses.

Rodeo prizes

▶ Champion rodeo riders can win prizes worth thousands of dollars. The prizes for many events are gold or silver belt buckles or beautifully made leather saddles.

The highly-trained horse

Horses under the "big top"

Like many animals, horses enjoy an audience. Applause excites them and they bask in admiration. Circus horses are no exception.

Circus horses fall into three groups. Liberty horses perform without being touched by humans. They are often part Arab and are chosen for their colouring, which is normally white or Palomino (chestnut with flaxen mane and tail).

High school horses are ridden in the ring and need two years' training to master the difficult movements they perform. They are usually Thoroughbreds. Bareback riders need a special kind of horse called a Rosinback. It can be of any breed but must have a broad, level back and a smooth canter.

The movements of the horses of the Spanish Riding School in Vienna look almost impossible. This is "haute école" or high school training at its most skilled. In the past, a man's fate in battle could depend on the understanding between him and his horse. Horses were sometimes trained to perform movements which might save their riders from difficult situations. The art of haute école has developed from these actions.

▶ Highly-trained Liberty horses perform at the Moscow State Circus.

The Spanish riding school

◀ A Lippizaner mare with her foal. The horses used at the Spanish Riding School are Lippizaners, a breed which goes back to 1580. Its ancestors were mainly Spanish Andalusians. All white horses are born black and gradually change to white as they grow older.

▶ A young stallion's first lessons at the Spanish Riding School are taught on the long rein. At this stage, the horse learns to trust its trainer and respond to simple commands. More difficult work begins later and the complete training takes many years.

The smallest horses in the world

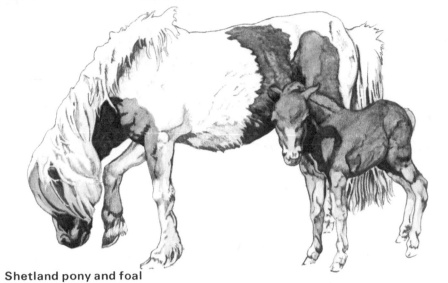

Shetland pony and foal

Falabella

▲ A Shetland mare with her foal. These appealing little ponies are only about 965 mm. (38 ins.) tall and are great favourites with circus audiences. They are usually trained to perform like Liberty horses.

▲ The Falabella pony is even smaller than the Shetland. An adult may only be 711 mm. (28 ins.) tall. These ponies come from South America and are much in demand for circuses and shows. They may be any colour but are often spotted.

◄ Princess Anne carries out a dressage test on the Queen's horse Columbus. Dressage shows the rider's degree of control over his or her horse. It is a version of haute ecole but less difficult.

Courbette

Capriole

◄ The *Courbette* is one of the most difficult movements performed by horses. The stallion lifts his forelegs off the ground and takes two or three leaps forward on his hind legs. Only a few stallions are capable of carrying out this exercise.

► In the *Capriole*, the horse leaps in the air with his forelegs tucked beneath him and kicks out with his hindlegs. This was originally taught to war horses. They could rescue their riders from difficulty, and at the same time aim a kick at any pursuers.

Sport on horseback

▲ This Turkish miniature shows horsemen hunting with falcons and with bows and arrows. Hunting is the oldest and most widespread form of horse sport.

▶ A tent-pegging contest in 1875. The rider must pull a tent peg from the ground with a lance while riding at a gallop, which is extremely difficult.

▼ Pig-sticking in India in the 19th century. This form of hunting was fast, exciting and often dangerous, as the wild boar is a fierce creature when cornered.

▲ A modern polo match. This sport demands a great deal from a pony. It must be very fast, aggressive and instantly obedient to the commands of its rider.

Keeping in trim

Mounted games are almost as old as the art of riding itself. But thousands of years ago men had little time for sport and there was a good reason behind the origins of most games on horseback.

Many games were developed by armies as training exercises for their cavalry. It was essential that horse and rider should act as one in a battle and that the horse should not be easily startled. They also had to be able to stop suddenly, to move off fast and to turn fast in tiny spaces. For all these qualities, mounted games were good training.

An international game

A very early horse sport was polo. It was being played over 2,000 years ago in Eastern Asia and probably began in Persia. Polo is an exciting game which requires courage and skill from horse and rider. Most polo ponies today come from South America, where their ancestors were the strong, agile horses of the gauchos.

Trotters and *troikas*

Not all horse sports are for mounted riders. Harness racing has been popular for many years in Russia and America and is gradually spreading.

Trotting is a form of harness racing in which the horse never moves out of a trot. Usually they race between the shafts of a two-wheeled vehicle called a sulky, but in Russia races are also held in the snow and the horses pull sledges called *troikas*.

▼ An American trotter in full racing turn-out. The horses are usually Standardbreds. The driver sits right behind the horse in the tiny, lightweight sulky.

Saddle pad

Reins

Handhold

Breast collar

Girth

Shaft

Sulky

Wheel disc

Knee boots

Quarter boot

Shin boots

▼ An exciting moment in a game of *bouzkachi* in Afghanistan. This is a fast and very rough sport in which the riders try to snatch the body of a dead goat from one another.

In the limelight the show jumper

Training from an early age

Show-jumping is one of the few sports in which men and women compete on equal terms. This is because success does not depend on strength. Good hands, patience, understanding and hard work are more important.

Riders usually come into top class show jumping via the juvenile classes and great importance is attached to children's events. Many children start by competing in small shows and in novice classes. A good season in the show ring may put them firmly in the front line of riders and open the way to a hard but thrilling career.

Cunning versus courage

Horses are often natural jumpers and many really enjoy show jumping. The ones that reach the top are those that combine ability and enjoyment. Some may like outdoor arenas, while others prefer the excitement of indoor shows, but in ability they usually fall into one of two groups.

Horses with great courage and determination do best in *puissance*, or high-jump, competitions. Those which are lithe and cunning as cats, and which can cut corners and hop over obstacles from any angle, are successful in speed contests.

▲ As the horse approaches a fence, it gathers its hind legs under its body in preparation to lifting its forelegs off the ground.

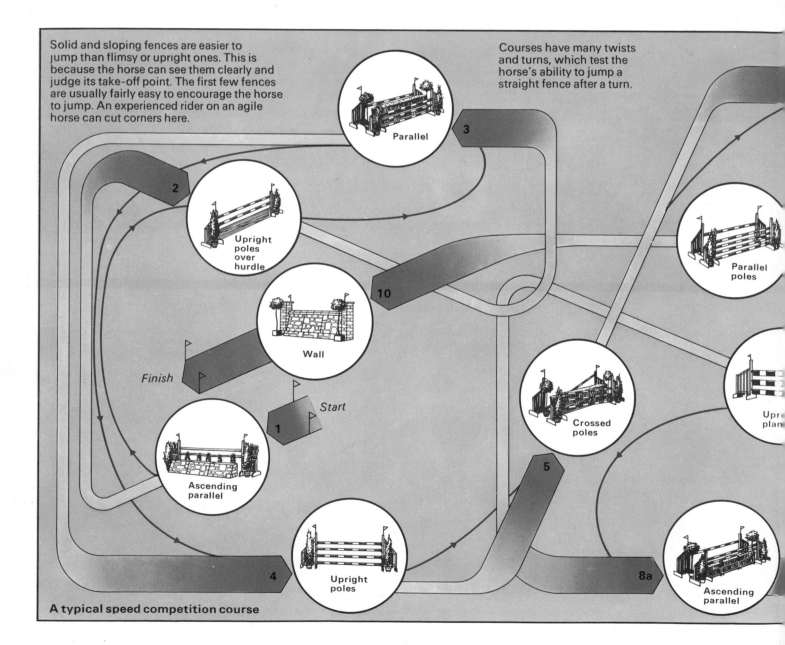

Solid and sloping fences are easier to jump than flimsy or upright ones. This is because the horse can see them clearly and judge its take-off point. The first few fences are usually fairly easy to encourage the horse to jump. An experienced rider on an agile horse can cut corners here.

Courses have many twists and turns, which test the horse's ability to jump a straight fence after a turn.

Parallel

3

2

Upright poles over hurdle

Parallel poles

10

Wall

Finish

Start

Crossed poles

Upr plan

1

5

Ascending parallel

4

Upright poles

8a

Ascending parallel

A typical speed competition course

▲ The horse must see the fence clearly to judge its take-off point. Hindquarters give the thrust necessary to clear the jump.

▲ The horse brings its weight forward to lift the hindquarters. As it jumps, the rider is well forward in the saddle.

▲ Forelegs are tucked well under to clear the top of the jump. The horse stretches its neck out in order to keep its balance.

▲ Horse and rider land correctly. Again, the horse uses its head to keep its balance, raising it until it moves on.

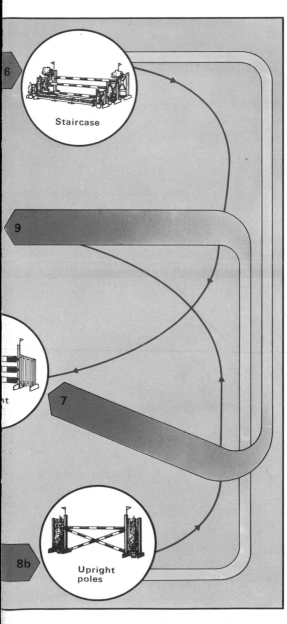

Staircase

Upright poles

◀ Plan of a speed competition course in an indoor arena. It is designed to test the jumping ability and speed of each competitor. The broad red line shows the track which would be taken by a novice horse and rider. The dotted line shows short cuts for a more experienced rider.

▲ Show jumper Harvey Smith takes a jump in fine style. His forward position in the saddle is slightly exaggerated, but this ensures that his weight is well over the horse's forehand while it jumps. His horse is on a short rein, so that he can keep a close but light contact with its mouth.

The world of racing

Racing in the 18th century. The jockeys ride with long stirrups and sit upright. Early artists could not draw galloping, so they tried to show the speed by making them look like rocking horses.

▲ Riding "like a monkey on a stick". This is the modern racing seat, with short stirrups and knees drawn up. It was introduced by Tod Sloan, an American rider, in the late 19th century. At speed, the jockeys crouch over the necks of their horses.

▲ Weighing in after a race. Horses are made to carry a certain weight, depending on how good they are. If the jockey is too light, lead weights are put under the saddle.

Enjoyment for everyone

Racing is a sport with a long history. There is a great difference between the rough and ready bareback contests of ancient Greece and the highly-organized sport of today, but the principle is the same.

An exciting race between two or more powerful animals and their skilful riders can be enjoyed by people of every type. It does not matter if they are rich or poor, and it is not necessary to know a great deal about horses. People also enjoy betting large sums of money on the possible results. This has made racing unpopular with the church and with governments in the past.

Until the 18th century, races were only run on flat ground, but then the steeplechase became popular. This race was so called because it was originally run from church steeple to church steeple, jumping whatever obstacles were in the path.

Checking for cheating

Also in the 18th century, many of the modern racing societies were founded. These were set up to organize the sport and to draw up rules. Racing was renowned for cheating of every sort. Horses were sometimes poisoned, and jockeys often took money to lose a race. Nowadays, there is a careful check on every stage of a race.

Breeding racehorses has become a science. In the past, all sorts of different horses would run together, but it was soon seen that Arab horses crossed with English breeds were the most successful. This led to the careful breeding of the modern Thoroughbred horse, which races throughout the world.

Ribot

Taking a photo finish picture

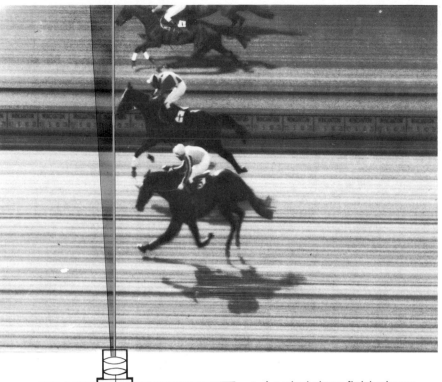

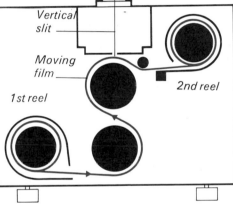

Vertical slit

Moving film

1st reel

2nd reel

▲ A typical photo finish picture. Human eyesight is not good enough to spot the winner in a close finish, so a photograph is taken. The top portion of the photograph is reflection in a mirror. This ensures that no horse is hidden behind another.

◄ How a photo finish camera works. The camera is mounted slightly above the finish and on a line with it. A continuously moving film passes across a vertical slit behind the lens. As each horse crosses the finishing line, its image is recorded.

The Thoroughbred

The Darley Arabian

◄ Ribot, one of the greatest racehorses of modern times. He was an Italian horse which was foaled in England in 1952. He won all his 16 races in Europe and then earned his keep by siring, or fathering, foals in England and the U.S. Many of his offspring inherited his great qualities and became successful racehorses.

► The Darley Arabian, a famous 18th century Arab racehorse, from whom Ribot was descended. All Thoroughbreds can trace their ancestors back to one of three great Arabian stallions: the Darley Arabian, the Byerley Turk and the Godolphin Arabian. They were all three bought by Englishmen and crossed with English mares.

Projects how to draw a horse

Perhaps you would like to draw horses and ponies. At first, this may seem very difficult as your subject will very rarely be quite still. At each movement the horse's body will change and its coat will take on a slightly different pattern of light and shade.

All animals are made up of intricately connected parts and organs. These form a unit made up of different basic shapes. When you start to draw horses, try to think of their bodies in these basic shapes and do not try to start by drawing an outline.

▶ Moving horses are quite difficult to draw. The pattern of movement of the legs changes from gait to gait. Before the camera was invented, people found it almost impossible to draw galloping horses. Their legs were moving so fast that they could never get them in the right position. If you look at old prints of horses racing, you will see that they look like rocking horses.

These drawings show a pony which is trotting. If you wish to draw a pony going faster or slower, try to find a photograph which shows the movement of the legs.

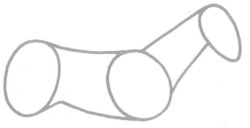

▲ First draw three basic shapes for the head, the fore quarters and the hind quarters. Connect them to form the body and neck.

▶ To draw a pony coming towards you, start off with basic shapes for the head and body. Indicate the tops of the legs.

▼ Draw in the neck to connect the head and body. Add the hind quarters to one side of your body shape and draw in the legs.

▲ Once you have the basic shapes, you can draw an outline of the whole body and the legs.

▲ Next, fill in the features of the face and the mane, tail and hooves. Lightly shade in the legs on the far side of the body.

▲ When you have an outline, you can add the tail, hooves and face. Shade in the drawing to show the curves and angles of the body.

▶ More shading can be added to show muscles and to give an idea of a shining coat.

▲ The final stage is to shade in your drawing.

▶ One of the most common sights in the country is a horse grazing. Use shapes again to show the position of the horse. Add some grass or hay to the finished drawing to give it a base.

▲ Many people like to make studies of the heads of horses. For these, you only need two basic shapes for head and neck. Draw a more detailed outline over the top of these shapes and then carefully set in the ears, eyes and muzzle and a silky mane.

Approaching a strange horse

Horses are naturally friendly creatures and, like humans, they enjoy attention. If you are approaching a horse you do not know, there are a few facts you should remember.

Never come up to a horse from behind or stand too close behind him. He may react instinctively to what he imagines to be danger and lash out with his hind legs. A blow from a horse's hoof can be very painful.

Do not give him titbits unless you have permission from the owner to do so. Ponies, especially, can become very bad-tempered if a titbit is not produced when they have learned to expect one.

If you are allowed to offer a titbit, choose a quartered apple or a carrot sliced lengthways. Place it on the flat of your palm and hold out your hand to him. Never hold the offering in your fingers or he might take them as well.

Avoid a horse which lays back his ears as you approach. It is a sign that he might bite.

How to describe a horse's colour

bay any shade of brown from light tan to dark brown, with black mane and tail.

black a true black with no light areas.

brown a dark brown with lighter areas, usually at the muzzle or around the eyes.

chestnut any light brown from pale gold to reddish-tan with mane and tail the same colour or lighter.

dun a yellowish-grey or yellowish-brown with dark mane and tail and usually a dark stripe along the backbone.

grey any shade of white to dark grey; a fleabitten grey is one that is slightly speckled.

palomino a chestnut with much paler mane and tail.

piebald black and white.

roan any solid colour with white hairs mixed in throughout. Brown with white is called a strawberry roan; black with white is a blue roan.

skewbald brown and white.

sorrel a light chestnut.

white used only to describe an albino horse, one with no pigmentation at all. Albinos have pink skin and eyes.

Books to read

Books about horses are so numerous that there are a few bookshops which sell nothing else. The best known of these is:

J.A. Allen & Co. Ltd.
(The Horseman's Bookshop)
1 Lower Grosvenor Place,
Buckingham Palace Road,
London SW1 0EL

who will send you a catalogue if you write to them. A large number of books are also available by post from:

Horse Books Ltd.
1 Tahoma Lodge,
Lubbock Road,
Chislehurst,
Kent BR7 5JS

General Reading

They Rode into Europe by Miklós Jankovich (Harrap). This tells the story of the spread of Eastern horses and horsemanship throughout Europe.

A History of Horsemanship by Charles Chenevix-Trench (Longman). A study of the evolution of different riding styles.

Man on Horseback by Glen Vernam (Harper & Row). This tells the story of the rider and his equipment through the ages.

The World's Finest Horses and Ponies edited by Richard Glyn (Harrap). A description of 200 different breeds of horse and pony with colour plates.

Specialized

Tourney and Joust by Steven Jeffreys (a Wayland Sentinel book). This is a well illustrated history of the tournament.

The Horse World of London (1893) by W.J. Gordon (J.A. Allen). A reprint of a book published in the 1890's about the enormous horse population of London and its work.

Salute the Carthorse by Philip A. Wright (Ian Allan). A tribute to the heavy breeds of horse.

Saddles and Spurs by Mary Lund and Raymond W. Settle (Bonanza). A vivid account of the short-lived Pony Express in the U.S.

There is a wide range of fiction about horses. Two books which have now become classics are *Black Beauty* by Anna Sewell, which is the autobiography of a Victorian carriage horse, and *National Velvet* by Enid Bagnold, the story of a young girl who rides the winner of the Grand National.

The Pony Club

About 100,000 young riders throughout the world belong to an organization called the Pony Club. The Pony Club was started in Great Britain in 1929 and now has branches in 25 countries ranging from Australia to Zambia.

The aims of the Club are to encourage children to ride, to look after their ponies properly and to enjoy all forms of sport connected with horses. You do not have to own a pony in order to join. Many members live in towns and ride at riding schools because they are unable to keep a pony.

The Club arranges many outings such as visits to studs and racing stables, film shows, picnics and parties. Members are also expected to attend instructional rallies.

Ordinary membership is open to anyone aged 16 years or under. Associate membership is for young people aged from 17 to 20. The annual subscription is £1.50.

If you are interested in becoming a member and would like to know the address of your nearest branch, write to:

The Secretary,
The Pony Club Headquarters,
National Equestrian Centre,
Stoneleigh,
Kenilworth,
Warwickshire CV8 2LR

Glossary

aged horse or pony over 8 yrs old.

aids the means by which a rider indicates his commands to a horse; hands, legs, body and voice are natural aids; whip and spurs are artificial aids.

bit part of the bridle which fits into the horse's mouth.

bridle headgear of the horse.

colt a young male horse.

dressage movements performed by a highly-trained horse.

fault show jumping error such as knocking down a fence, refusing to jump or falling.

feather hair on a horse's leg.

filly a young female horse.

foal baby horse from birth until its first birthday.

gait movement of a horse.

gelding a castrated male horse.

girth strap which passes under the horse's belly and holds the saddle in place.

hand unit of measurement equal to 102 mm. (4 ins.).

haute école a French term meaning high school: movements performed by very highly-trained horses.

mare an adult female horse.

stallion male horse used for breeding.

stud place where stallions used for breeding are kept.

turn-out general appearance of horse and rider.

yearling young horse between the ages of one and two years old.

Index

Illustration Credits
Key to the positions of illustrations: (T) top, (C) centre
(B) bottom and combinations; for example (TR) top right,
or (CL) centre left.

Artists
John Bolton: 11 (T), 32-3, 36-7
Peter Connolly: 8-9
Ron Hayward Associates: 12-13, 14 (T)
Jim Long: 24-5
John Martin and Artists Ltd.:
        T. Crosby-Smith: 4-5, 14-15, 28-9, 39
        W. Francis Phillips: 22-3, 34
Ken Mitchell: 27, 44-5
Tony Payne: 18-19
Colin Rose: 11 (C & B), 13 (T), 24 (T), 26, 32 (T), 40-1, 43

Photographs and prints
American Saddle Horse Breeders Ass.: 33 (TL)
Australian News & Information Bureau: 22 (BR)
Bodleian Library: 10 (C)
Martin Chillmaid: 3 (L)
Findlay Davidson: 37 (C)
P. Dean: 17

Fores Ltd.: 43 (B)
Forestry Commission: 29 (C)
Sonia Halliday: 30, 38 (TL)
Robert Harding Ass.: 39
Mansell Collection: 3 (R), 7, 26 (C), 42 (T)
Mary Evans Picture Library: 8, 10 (T), 12, 38 (TR & C)
Museum of the American Indian: 33 (C)
National Coal Board: 26 (B)
National Film Board of Canada: 22 (BL)
H. Pasmore: 20-1
Pictor Ltd.: 23, 26 (T), 27 (B), 28, 31 (BL), 36 (T & B)
Planet News: 10 (BR)
Production Television Rencontre: 10 (BR)
Quarter Horse Association: 33 (TR)
Racing Information Bureau: 42 (C & BL), 43 (TR)
Radio Times Hulton Picture Library: 14
Peter Roberts: 29 (T & B), 35 (C & B), 38 (B)
Rodeo Information Foundation: 35 (TR)
Royal Horse Society of Iran: 31 (R)
N. Scott: 25
Sport & General: 41, 42 (BR)
Starr-Duffy Studios: 42-3 (C)
Sally Ann Thompson: 18
Western Americana: 34